A
Bed's Eye
View

Prayers for those who are unwell
- at home or in hospital

ANDREW WYLIE

A BED'S EYE VIEW

First published 2012 by
The Wellrose Press
Peat Inn, Fife, Scotland KY15 5LH
www.bedseyeview.co.uk

in association with
Breathing Space Productions

ISBN 978 0 9565894 1 5

Also by Andrew Wylie:

Just Being There - With Bears & Tigers in the North Sea
2006 - Dunedin Academic Press
ISBN 1 903765 41 2

A
Bed's Eye
View

ANDREW WYLIE

✝

The left-hand pages have been left blank—
Like me you will have insights and they can
make these prayers come alive for you.
If you write them down, this book can become
a very personal source of strength and support.

Andrew Wylie

A Bed's Eye View

About Andrew

I cannot move, but I can smile and
show my gratitude.

It's through the simplest of signs
another's load is lightened.

– words from Andrew's prayer "How weak I am"

These prayers and thoughts grew out of a stay in
hospital, and so are very real, and may be of
help both to anyone who is unwell and also to
friends and relatives as they try to understand.
The prayers have immense strength and insight
as they come out of suffering, as true prayer often
does.

Andrew Wylie was an amazing and remarkable
person. I was privileged to know him in just the
last 25 years of his life, including his last few weeks
on earth when he was able to look calmly at death
and beyond.

He was ordained as a Church of Scotland minister
in 1953 but found that while he could respect the
boundaries of parish life they were too restricting
for him, and so he was always ready to push aside
the barriers and move into the places where people
lived and worked.

This happened throughout his life but is most
clearly seen in the two chaplaincies he began
during his ministry. The first to the shops
and offices around the fashionable church in
Edinburgh's New Town of which he was minister
and, the second, to the men and women working
in the oil and gas industries of the North Sea. He
discovered that no Church made provision for
them and so offered to attempt to do so, moving to
Aberdeen and a completely new work.

Andrew saw Jesus going beyond the religious boundaries of Galilee and he sought to do the same as the opportunity came to him. In doing so he brought great blessings to many, many people.

This book of prayers is a continuation of his reaching out. Not content to just be in hospital himself he wanted to be of help to those he met and those who would follow him there.

I especially like the prayer for his fellow patients. He says –

Help me to think of them.
Their fears are just like mine.
Time and shared experience
Should bring us close together...

But if communication fails
And friendship falters,
Then at the very least
Let me be helpful by my quiet understanding
Of my companions.

It is a stating of the approach Andrew took in the North Sea, and which I witnessed in awe. He summed it up in the title of the book he wrote about a chaplain's life on the oil platforms – *Just Being There.*

Andrew died of cancer in the summer of 2011, without fear, and it was his hope that this book will be of a help to anyone who is ill.

It probably will as it has been written by someone who has been there.

Gerald Stranraer-Mull
Dean Emeritus of the Diocese of Aberdeen and Orkney

For a Testing Time

My God, I am so scared
As much afraid that I will show my fear
As fear itself.
Help me to understand that courage
Is the control and conquering of fear.
My resolution is so thin,
My frailty so plain.
Grant me trust in healing hands.
And, if the signs of overwork are shown
In gruffness and sharp tongues
Make me more thankful
For those whose skills serve me.
If I can fight my fear
The helpers can be helped,
They also have their testing times.

*Even gold passes through the assayers'
fire, and more precious than perishable gold
is faith which has stood the test. The trials
come so that our faith may prove itself worthy
of all praise, glory and honour when Jesus
Christ is revealed.*

1 Peter 1, v. 7.

1

Why Me?

Good Lord, still good,
Although my confidence is shaken in your goodness.
I have heard about this place
But now I know it first hand,
Help me to profit from the days ahead,
Be they many or quite few.
May I learn from each experience.
Then, when I am recovered and more strong,
I shall be more able to cope with myself,
And those I love.
In this way I shall lead a life
So much more enriched.
Teach me ..... Good Lord.

Man's ways are not of his own choosing.
Nor is it for a man to determine his
course in life. Correct us, O Lord, but with
justice, not in anger.

Jeremiah 10, vv. 23-24.

For the One at Home

To you, Lord God, I commit the one I love;
Who now must cope alone;
Living for the present though anxious for
the future.
Be with my beloved.
Once seemingly secure in plans we made,
But all to be re-cast.
Alone, with responsibilities once shared,
And high hopes now brought low.
May this remembrance
Be the best spur in my sickness.
To keep the discipline of mind and body
That helps the healing, and once found,
Maintains it.

H*elp one another to carry these heavy
loads, and in this way you will fulfil the
law of Christ.*

Galatians 6, v. 2.

Give Me Patience

Lord, I am impatient
Upon my back.
I want to be
Up on my feet
And feel fit.
I must be patient and do what I am told to do;
But time seems stopped.
I lie alert to every beat of heart;
To every throb of pulse;
To every tug of muscle;
Ache of bone.
Make me look out, not in.
Preserve me from this restlessness of mind,
This self concern.
Then I shall stand on my two feet.

May the Lord direct your hearts towards God's love, and the steadfastness of Christ.

2 Thessalonians 3, v. 5.

When I am Afraid

Father in Heaven, it's hard to pretend
I am not beset
By numerous, nameless, fears.
But what is life
If it is not uncertainty?
And what is sickness
If not a time to draw
On strength of spirit
To offset the weakness of the flesh?
That's how Christ came through.
It's my path too.

L et us fix our eyes on Jesus, the author and
perfector of our Faith, who for the joy set
before him, endured the cross, scorning its
shame, and sat down at the right hand of the
throne of God.

Hebrews 12, v. 2.

When I am Tired

It's strange to lie in bed
Yet grow more weary.
To feel a heaviness
Of eye and arm.
To sense the mind drifting
Far from concentrated thought.
Make me relax
And sink into calm repose.
Then you take charge O God.
And from this rest
Will come the strength
To meet another day.

Come to me, all you who are weary and
burdened, and I will give you rest. Take
my yoke upon you and learn of me, for I am
gentle and humble in heart, and you will find
rest for your souls. For my yoke is easy and my
burden is light.

Matthew. 11, vv. 28-30

How Weak I Am

When in Church I have often heard it said
Your strength is made perfect in my weakness.
These words must now be true.
I lie dependent on another
Who meets my every need.
I am renewed.
I cannot move, but I can smile
And show my gratitude.
It's through the simplest of signs
Another's load is lightened.
Even when helpless
I shall not be hopeless.
Though I am weak yet I am strong.
It's your strength.

M*y grace is all you need; power comes to
its full strength in weakness.*

2 Corinthians 12, v. 9.

Oh, To Be Alone!

Heavenly Father,
I remember how your Son loved men,
And was often in their midst.
But I remember too
The times when He sought solitude.
There are times when,
Surrounded by my fellows,
Unable, even for a moment, to be alone
And speak to you -
I long for that stillness
That makes your presence real,
And for that quiet
When I can hear your word.
Let me not forget that you are here,
In the busyness
A still, small voice.

*For I am convinced that there is nothing in
death or life, nothing in all creation that
can separate us from the love of God in Christ
Jesus our Lord.*

Romans 8, vv. 38-39.

All Things New

Unchanging God, how I have changed.
New insights show me more about myself,
And of this world.
I know how I can be afraid,
Yet how my fear is overcome.
I know I am more religious than I might admit,
Or than my closest friends might dare to think;
I know my need of you.
Not as a prop,
But as an explanation of those basic things,
That mean so much.
Life and its purpose;
Death and its mystery;
Pain and its weariness;
Joy and its uplifiting.
Father, may all things be new, always,
At all times.

A man who is unspiritual refuses what belongs
to the Spirit of God; it is folly to
him; he cannot grasp it, because it needs to be
judged in the light of the Spirit.

1 Corinthians 2, v. 14.

So Much Care

Almighty God, how humbling,
Daily routine continues whether I am
present or not,
But some have more to do because I am not there.
And some have work to do which is quite new.
Others may know a respite from the everyday.
Within my heart
There is much gratitude for loyalty of colleagues,
Understanding of employers,
And the great concern of all my friends.
All this
I took too much for granted,
Sometimes grumbled at,
And never tried to understand.
Forgive me.

A friend is a loving companion at all times,
and a brother is born to share troubles.

Proverbs 17, v.17

When I Cannot Sleep

God, I lie awake;
Night noises seem so magnified,
A sleeper's breath so deep,
And I am envious.
My mind alert
Scans problems, real and fanciful.
There is a loneliness at night,
But others know this too.
Make me think of them,
And not just of myself.
Then as I lie awake,
Grant me the quiet mind,
And trusting heart,
That come from thoughts that rise to you;
Then I shall know your peace.

*J*esus said, *"Peace is my parting gift to you, my
own peace, such as the world cannot give".*

John 14, v. 27.

The Kindness of Others

Forgiving Lord, this is a prayer of shame.
Upon this planet Earth
It's hard to recognise true kindness,
And harder still to show it.
But this place is a smaller world.
The superficial stands revealed.
Deeds of kindness and goodwill abound.
Here, people think of one another.
I am disturbed by my small thoughts
For I still doubt the motives of my fellow men.
Praise God! For now I am enriched.
Fresh insights have appeared,
As I begin to lose myself
For someone else,
And, in the process, find myself.

B*y gaining his life a man will lose it; by
losing his life for my sake, he will gain it.*

Matthew 10, v. 39.

For Fellow Patients

Lord, they are quite unknown to me;
Their names, their jobs, or how they pass
their time.
Yet they are just the same as me,
Anxious and afraid.
Help me to think of them.
Their fears are just like mine.
Time and shared experience
Should bring us close together.
So guide my thoughts and theirs,
From bleakness into light,
From common woes to common hopes.
But if communication fails
And friendship falters,
Then at the very least
Let me be helpful by my quiet understanding
Of my companions.

*He comforts us in all our troubles, so
that we in turn may be able to comfort
others in any trouble of theirs and to share with
them the consolation we ourselves receive from
God.*

2 Corinthians 1, v. 4.

When Unpleasant
and Unfriendly

Father in heaven, you sent your Son
To show the likeness that is yours.
How unlike Him we are!
Grumbling and groaning at our lot.
Accepting all things as our right and due.
Through our impatience, and ill temper.
Showing a restless spirit, and a troubled mind,
When I am like this - forgive.
And help me to show more
Humour to the humourless,
And grace to the graceless.
The likeness of Christ is shown when
wounding words
Are turned to good.
Then healing starts again.
This is one way that I can help.

As we have worn the likeness of the man
made dust, so shall we wear the likeness
of the heavenly man.

1 Corinthians 15, v. 49.

The Great Adventure

Father, the mystery of death can come so close,
Suddenly the partition between this life
And the life to come,
Can seem so frail.
The body can become a husk,
The spirit freed to venture
Through the valley of the shadow
To its homecoming.
Suddenly, I see
That things unseen
Matter much more
Than things I can
Taste and touch and hold.
I now understand in this life we hold a
stewardship,
But only to prepare us
For the one to come.

When our mortality has been clothed
with immortality, then the saying of
scripture will come true: "Death is swallowed
up; victory is won."

1 Corinthians 15, v. 54.

What Can I Learn?

That in my plight
Trust is full commitment
Into the care of those
With understanding skill.
That Faith looks to the light
When others cannot see
Beyond the grey.
That hope knows setbacks
And is not overcome
By weakness of the body.
My God! My Faith, and Hope,
Is placed in you.
For in the Word made Flesh
The tears, perplexity and pain
Were Christ's.
Yet His was the victory.
Now it can be mine.

I am convinced that there is nothing in death or life, in the realm of spirits or superhuman powers, in the world as it is, or the world as it shall be, in the forces of the universe, in heights or depths - nothing in all creation that can separate us from the love of God in Christ Jesus our Lord.

Romans 8, vv. 38-39.

For Those In Charge

Dear Lord, I know
That behind the anonymity of uniform
Is found a person;
Full of hopes, fears, and frustrations.
Make me to open my eyes
At so much concern for so many.
In contrast to my own preoccupation with myself.
I see the confidence
That comes from training.
The poise from purpose.
May I never forget that
Behind the strength and competence
On which I lean so much
There is a person.
With the same pressures, joys and sorrows,
That are my lot.

*You, like the lamp, must shed light among
your fellows, so that, when they see the
good you do, they may give praise to your
Father in heaven.*

Matthew 5, v. 16.

A Prayer For The Doctors

Heavenly Father, make me accept
That in their hands
Rests the design for my recovery.
Make me accept the daily steps
Set out to make me well.
Make me appreciate their tirelessness;
For they appear at all times
Day or night.
Make me acknowledge their real concern
Which makes me feel
A person, not a thing.
Which makes me co-operate
In all things asked of me.
Then their skill,
Matched by my intent
Must give me hope.

His heart warms all the more to you as he recalls how ready you all were to do what he asked, meeting him as you did in fear and trembling. How happy I am now to have complete confidence in you.

2 Corinthians 7, vv. 15-16.

A Prayer For The Nurses

Lord God, forgive
My muddle.
A collar or a different coloured shoulder
strap
May not mean much to me.
But can mean everything along a road of
training.
Responsibility comes that is beyond
The comprehension of their peers.
So too the crises
That determine life or death.
Although I may be older,
In some ways more experienced;
Yet this I know:
That from their patience, calm and
cheerfulness
I have so much to learn.

D*o not be conceited or think too highly of yourself; but think your way to a sober estimate based on the measure of faith that God has dealt to each of you.*

Romans 12, v. 3

The Helper's Prayer

God! That tortured body could be mine.
So often do I wonder "why the pain?"
Can it be there in the agony
That I shall glimpse a nobility of soul?
That in a mockery of flesh and bone
There is something sensed......not seen,
That does not die?
As I become aware of my mortality
Make me humbled by my good health.
A precious stewardship.
Use my healing skills
To cure, to comfort, and conduct
Through the barrier of pain,
To life itself.

*Seeing that we have been entrusted with
this commission, which we owe entirely to
God's mercy, we never lose heart.*

2 Corinthians 4, v. 1.

A Doctor's Prayer

Merciful God, although this patient is one of
many
To him I can mean much.
Illness is entirely personal,
And I must treat the man
As much as any malady.
If I am tired or harassed
Renew my spirit,
Lest by some word or action
I betray myself.
Guide me to that balance
That can make me professionally detached
Yet still giving something of myself.
So starts the healing link
Full forged when I begin
To treat the patient
As much as the complaint.

I *pray that your inward eyes may be*
illumined, so that you may know what is the
hope to which he calls you, and how vast the
resources of his power open to us who trust in
him.

Ephesians 1, vv. 18-19.

The Sister's Prayer

Strengthen me, good Lord, in watching over
Many beds,
Where no-one chose to lie.
Alert me! Good Lord,
For illness produces
Irritability and impatience.
Remind me! Good Lord,
That I do not see people
As they wish to be.
Help me! Good Lord,
To utter the reassuring word at the right time.
Guide me! Good Lord,
To be sure in all I do.
Calm me! Good Lord,
That my busyness does not become bustle.
So, uphold me, for though so frail
Your Spirit can make me strong.

Help only comes from the Lord, Maker of heaven and earth. How could he let your foot stumble? How could he, your guardian, sleep?

Psalm 121, vv. 2-3.

For New Arrivals

Dear Lord, unchanging, in a changing world.
Now I pray for those whose plans
Have not been fulfilled.
Folk who have left home, and not returned.
Whose bed is not their own, but such as this.
Victims of sudden illness or accident,
Shattered by circumstance,
Yet, not too ill to sense they may not be
The same again.
We pray for loved ones shocked by
unexpected news.
Beset by new anxieties and new concerns.
We remember them in routine gone awry.
In situations needing calm and courage.
Girdle both sick and well
With your unchanging love.

Jesus said, "I am not alone, because the Father
is with me. I have told you all this so that in
me you may find peace. In the world you will
have trouble. But courage! The victory is mine;
I have conquered the world."

John 16, v. 33.

A Prayer At Visiting Time

Dear Lord,
However I may feel,
Grant me optimism and serenity
To reassure all those who
In their kindness come to me.
Forgive my weariness
With those who overstay
Their time at my bedside.
Give to them a sensitivity
Towards my longing for a word alone
With those I love the most.
Make me grateful for
The tokens of affection I receive,
Save me from the cynicism
That can spoil a gift
Sincerely offered.

When I was ill you came to my help.

Matthew 25, v. 36.

When Others Go Home

Now I need new friends!
This is the time that old ones
Are restored and can go home.
Dear Lord, control my envy,
Slack my sense of grievance
That some have not been here as long as I.
Free me from self pity.
Make me be glad for them
And those they love.
May all who leave this place
Have the will to get well,
And the mind to accept
The wise advice given.
May I do the same
.... when my time comes.

G od himself has said, "I will never leave you
or desert you"; and so we can take courage
and say, "The Lord is my helper, I will not
fear."

Hebrews 13, v.6.

For Those Who Return
To An Empty Home

Father of all families,
There are some whose welcome
Will be an empty room.
A cold hearth.
I pray for those for whom loneliness
Is all too familiar.
Make me more mindful
Of those who have no-one.
More ready to offer fellowship
To those by themselves.
Better prepared to communicate
The promise of Christ's presence,
Everywhere.

L ook the hour is now coming, has indeed already come, when you are all to be scattered, each to his home, leaving me alone. Yet I am not alone, because the Father is with me.

John 16, v.32.

On Going Home

Good God, it will be fine
To feel the wind upon my face.
To see green grass.
To be in my own room
With things I know so well;
To laugh with those I love.
But when I leave this place,
And say goodbye;
Help me to speak
A word of help and strength
To those who stay behind.
May all whose skill has set me right
Know my thanksgiving.
Not merely for regained strength,
But also for lessons learned
From those who, serving others,
Serve your Son.

Jesus, rose from the table, laid aside his
garments, and taking a towel, tied it round
him. Then he poured water into a basin, and
began to wash his disciples' feet and to wipe
them with the towel.

John 13, vv. 3-5.

- Notes -

These brief prayers are the result of a few
weeks in hospital, but many of them are
relevant to those who are ill at home.
Hospitalisation was a new experience for the
author and, in retrospect, a source of much
enrichment and personal growth. Nothing
can take away the hopes and fears that flood
through a patient during this demanding
experience. But there are insights to be
gained. Faith can be discovered or renewed
and His word can come alive. In short,
illness can be a time of opportunity – be
positive and use it!

Andrew Wylie

The Wellrose Press
Peat Inn, Fife , Scotland KY15 5LH
www.bedseyeview.co.uk

in association with
Breathing Space Productions
Isle of Whithorn, Scotland DG8 8JD

£5.99

ISBN 978 0 9565894 1 5

9 780956 589415